STORMY ROAD
FOR THIS PILGRIM

Nelson O. Hayashida

A native Hawaiian, Nelson O. Hayashida is presently employed with the Hawaii Baptist Convention as the Baptist Campus Minister, University of Hawaii, Manoa. Listed in the 1976 *Who's Who Among Students in American Universities and Colleges* and the 1977 *Outstanding Young Men of America,* he previously served as pastor for congregations in Texas and California.

VANTAGE PRESS
New York   Washington   Atlanta   Hollywood

1978

Verses marked TLB are taken from *The Living Bible,*
copyright 1971 by Tyndale House Publishers, Wheaton,
Illinois. Used by permission.

FIRST EDITION

Published by Vantage Press, Inc.
516 West 34th Street, New York, New York 10001

Manufactured in the United States of America
Standard Book Number 533-03031-5

To my mother and father

whose union

I am

Contents

Preface

I'm writing this book to fulfill two needs. The first is the need for self-expression. Everyone needs self-expression, one form of which is the written word. Secondly, there is a gaping need for Asian-Americans to express themselves—through any medium.

Asian-Americans have been the victims of prejudice, discrimination, and unfair stereotyping. The kind of discriminatory practices against Asian-Americans, however, have been camouflaged to a greater degree than that with the blacks of America. Perhaps for this reason many are unaware of the unequal treatment frequently imposed upon Americans of Oriental descent. Asian-Americans do not like to be classified as second-class citizens any more than do other ethnic segments of society.

Asian-Americans, or those who are citizens of the United States and whose ancestry stems from the Orient, constitute a very small minority in this country. One reason for this has been past discriminatory immigration laws. It has been difficult for Asian-Americans to forcefully reveal unfair attitudes and practices when their number is so few.

Because of this lack of a powerful voice, then, and because by nature Orientals are not prone to rebel against "authority," it is easy to see why so many people are unfamiliar with, for example, the inexcusable act against Japanese-Americans during World War II. I am calling attention to the regrettable American tragedy which placed thousands of loyal Americans of Japanese lineage in concentration camps—this without due process of law, an act clearly unconstitutional and grossly immoral. In addition, the United States government confiscated or forced these innocents to practically "give away" their lands, property, and belongings—possessions which were obtained through years of hard work. After their release, many of these Americans were without jobs or a sense of direction. For the older folks it was traumatic to be released after years of deprivation and to pick up the pieces. For the children, they had a different set of problems. Every life was affected.

Racial hatred and scapegoating isn't unique to America, however. For example, during this same war the Jews suffered *unbelievably* in Germany. Historians can cite numerous other examples.

I point these things out not because I intend to write about my "beef" over the injustices done to Japanese-Americans, but simply because it is in this kind of (im)moral atmosphere and cultural milieu that I have been born and raised. I'm fortunate that I haven't endured many of the hardships others have. Truly, my heart cries for anyone who suffers unjustly.

My primary intention in writing is to tell you a little bit about myself. Partial familiarity, and hopefully greater understanding, of Americans of Oriental ancestry cannot but enhance better attitudes and relationships *by* and *with* Anglo-Americans. My great dream is that *we all* could live like brothers and sisters in this great land that is ours, however imperfect it may be.

I write as a Japanese-American. I recognize the fact that every person is a unique individual. That is, no one is a carbon copy of anyone else's physical, emotional, and psychological constitution. But I write with a set of experiences, feelings, and desires similar to that of other natural-born citizens of the continental United States who are of Japanese or Asian lineage. And indirectly, it is conceivable that other ethnic minorities in the continental United States may identify with some of the assertions in the pages to follow.

Those who are to identify with me most intimately, however, are Christians of Asian ancestry. I write this book as a Christian who, because of his ethnic minority status, has a few thoughts to share on the particular stresses and problems of a member of such a group in this country.

I have found not only my salvation but my help in Jesus Christ. Christ has revealed to me my "true identity," an essential and fundamental base from which I'm learning to cope with ethnic anxieties and gain victory over apparent defeat. In addition, it's my prayer that the remarks I make in challenging ethnic minority Christians and Anglo-American Christians will result in better understanding on the part of both—for it is only in unison that Christians can bear witness for God's greatest glory!

Introduction

Thank you for joining me in what I hope will be an enlightening experience. Some of you may be familiar with the plight of Asian-Americans in the United States. For others, the pages to follow may awaken you to new feelings and awareness. But I trust everyone will benefit from this book, a project of mine that began three years ago.

I want to introduce you to David Y. Hirano. He has graciously granted me permission to print his autobiography. The account to follow was originally published in the December (1976) and January (1977) issues of the *Pacific and Asian American Ministries Newsletter* (a United Church of Christ publication). Hirano's story serves as a keen insight into the Asian-American dilemma and therefore an appropriate introduction to this book.

* *

My father is Hiroshima-ken (*Ken* refers to the prefecture in which he was born). His lineage is of a *samurai* (a warrior, something like a knight). Until he was ten or so, he was reared by a governess because the family was wealthy. One day creditors came and possessed everything they had: money, clothes, house, land. A conniving and gambling Buddhist priest had forged my grandfather's seal and put it on his gambling debts. In one day the Hirano family was reduced from riches to, in my father's words, "beggary."

My grandfather came to Hawaii to work in the cane fields to make money so that the family could get back on its feet. It was difficult for people to leave Japan because the Japanese government wanted only the best people to leave. Thus, they had to meet stringent requirements in order to emigrate.

The Japanese were well liked in Hawaii because the Hawaiians thought they were like them. When my father was old enough, fifteen or sixteen, he left Japan to join my grandfather and my uncle. My father says that it was difficult for him to pass the physical before emigrating and the journey on board a small ship was full of hardship.

My father landed in Hilo on the Big Island of Hawaii where he lived at the Hilo Boarding School. Here he learned carpentry and English. He worked in the cane fields. The boarding school fed and clothed them. The Hawaii Congregational Conference ran the school.

It was at the Hilo Boarding School that my father was converted and received his call into the Christian ministry. He left the school for the mainland where he entered the Bible Institute of Los Angeles. Later, he transferred to another Bible College in Hollywood which is now a part of Azusa Pacific College.

After receiving his diploma, he with three others established the Japanese Holiness Denomination and founded the L.A. Holiness Church, the San Fernando Holiness Church, another in Tuscon, and still another in Modesto. The Holiness Church is not to be confused with the Pentecostal groups. The Japanese Holiness churches are Methodist in polity and Baptist in theology.

I know little about my mother's history. She is Nisei (that is second generation). Her parents (Isei, first generation in America) came to Hawaii to make money by working in the cane fields. While here, she was born, then shortly afterwards, having made their money, the family went back to Japan.

My mother was educated in Japan. The term that is used to describe my mother is *Kibei,* one who is born in the United States, goes back to Japan to be educated, and returns to the United States. My mother by birth in Hawaii inherited American citizenship. My father and mother met in L.A. while she was at the Bible college. They were married and together they "devoted their lives to the Lord."

They went to Japan. My father had a six-year-old son from a previous marriage and so the three went to Hamamatsu to establish a church there. I was born on a cold December evening. We lived in Hamamatsu until I was about two and a half years old. My sister was six months old when we moved to Hawaii. I was fluent in speaking Japanese when we landed in Hawaii.

The first four years in Hawaii are blurry in my memory. I remember family baths in my uncle's *furo-ba* (bath house); playing with my cousins, being disciplined by a strict father, going to kindergarten, and learning to write my name Yoshito.

At five, going on six, the trauma that shaped our lives took place. By this time, another child had been born into our family, so now there were three children, and my mother was very pregnant with another.

It was Sunday morning and we had gone to Sunday School about three miles from Pearl Harbor. In the midst of Sunday School we heard airplanes flying low overhead, and it seemed as though there were explosions everywhere, the sky was black with smoke.

We closed Sunday School and went home. My father turned on the radio and we heard: "Air raid, Air raid, Take cover, Take cover!" We had no place to go. I tried to hide under the table. We had lunch, but being so excited and scared, I got sick and vomited. It was a terrible day.

The days following the raid were busy with building bomb shelters, with gathering emergency provisions, with trying to normalize living, with blackouts and sirens wailing in the middle of the night. Seven days after the attack on Pearl Harbor my brother was born.

Then one day there was a knock on the door. I answered it and there stood two men with rifles at port arms. They asked me where my father was. I told them in the back yard. They asked me to get him, so I did. When he came in they told him to get his toothbrush and underwear and come with them. My father did as instructed, and that was the last we saw of him for the next four years.

In the meantime, my mother was left with a rebellious teen-age stepson, a one-month-old baby, two daughters, two and four years old and me, who had just turned six. Shortly before the war began my father affiliated with the Southern Baptists. They came to our aid. Since my mother had no means of support and we had no place to live, the Southern Baptists gave my mother $35.00 a month and a place to live. It wasn't much, a four-room shack (bedroom, living room, kitchen, and bath joined by a common porch) but it was a place to live.

The shack was in the upper-class part of Manoa and, therefore, the Caucasian section. We were the only Japanese family in the neighborhood. Schoolmates made it difficult for my half-brother and me because we were Japanese from Japan. I still bear physical scars from the rocks thrown at me.

My mother worked as a seamstress, I went to school, a woman sat with the other children until I came home and took over. My half-brother had gone to live with his grandmother.

There were nights of terror when the air raid sirens wailed and we would gather our possessions and make our way in the darkness to the community bomb shelters. There were gas mask tests and bomb shelter drills. Always there was the fear that we would be attacked again.

There were fun times, too, as the neighborhood children and we got acquainted and explored the neighborhood together. I felt no feelings of alienation from them because I was Japanese. They knew our circumstance and we benefited from their care and generosity.

The missionaries in our neighborhood were the only ones who would not let their children play with us. We could go to their homes for Royal Ambassadors, but we couldn't play with their children unless they snuck out to play with us. They lived in a beautiful house while we lived in a shack.

The American government told us that we had to get English names, so my uncle gave me the choice of Samuel or David. I chose David. Then the government said, "You ought not speak Japanese," so I didn't. In fact, I became so proficient at English that I passed a test and was allowed to go to English Standard Schools where it was bad to be Japanese. I did well at mimicking and trying to become white.

When my father returned we had difficulty adjusting. The missionary who lived close by and pastored my father's church during the war sold him his car which he bought before the war for $400.00 for the exact same price. A childless missionary couple came to Honolulu, and the Southern Baptist Convention built them a beautiful three bedroom house just a hundred yards from our shack. It seemed unjust.

Then we moved to a two bedroom house. It was better than the shack we had lived in. The neighborhood was also different. It was mixed. From age eleven to seventeen, my friends represented almost every nationality in Hawaii, two were Caucasians, two Japanese, a Korean-Hawaiian, and a Portuguese. These were the boys

I played with, got into trouble with, worked with, and fought with.

Throughout my childhood, my mother wanted me to go to college. She felt that this was the only way in which I would be able to make it in American Society. She implicitly told us that we had to be better than the *haoles* (Hawaiian for whites). The only way we would be able to stand up to the haole missionary was if we had a superior education.

When I was old enough, I sold papers and saved money for college. I chose Wake Forest College in North Carolina because it was a Southern Baptist college with good academic standing and away from Texas, Louisiana, and Mississippi where other Asian Southern Baptists from Hawaii were going. The missionaries protested to my father about my choice, but my father let me make my choice.

In my first 17 years I went from being Japanese to being an "American" and denying my Japaneseness. The war together with the intense persecution, with my father's internment and with the neighborhood in which I lived made a difference in my attitude about myself. I was fluent in Japanese until the war, but at eleven years of age, I was unable to speak it. Furthermore, when at twelve, I tried to learn Japanese, I blocked, and couldn't learn it. I had almost fully acculturated.

At 17, I went to Wake Forest College. This began a new phase of my life. I had been denying my identity and in North Carolina it was hard to deny it. Yet I was able to say I was Hawaiian and not admit to being Japanese. I rarely said my middle name and rarely wrote it. I had dual citizenship but I never claimed to be Japanese.

I was a minority of the minorities in North Carolina. There were only two other Orientals in the school and they were Japanese nationals. Occasionally we would get together and concoct a Japanese meal, but it was always makeshift and didn't taste like much.

My diet became the Southern diet. My talking was like a North Carolinian. My habits were anglicized. If it were not for the summers when I went to New York to live with my half-brother, I would not have had any meaningful contacts with anyone of my nationality throughout my college career.

In college, I proved I was an American. I enrolled in the ROTC program and in my freshman year became soldier of the year. I ran for student government offices and made every office I ran for. Eventually I became Student Government president.

Because I felt shy and because I didn't feel that any girl wanted to date me, because I felt inferior and because I was Japanese, I did little dating. When I became student body president I couldn't find a date for the homecoming game and I stood feeling humiliated before the homecoming crowd.

Because of the responsibilities I had as a child, I didn't play much. Away from my parents I learned to play in college. I didn't excel in academics, but otherwise I did okay.

I majored in Education and got my commission in the Infantry. I never went on active duty because I decided to go to seminary. I chose Andover Newton Theological School because I didn't like the exclusiveness of the Southern Baptists. Also, I wanted to go to school in the Boston area. Schools like Union were too expensive. I applied at Andover Newton and was accepted.

While in North Carolina, I had my first exposure to blacks. I couldn't understand why they were segregated; why they had to eat in certain places; why they were living in one section of the town. I noticed the politeness of the black person for the white, and the paternalistic niceness of "Good boy" from the whites to the blacks. It wasn't too different from the paternalism I was experiencing. I had difficulty understanding the treatment of blacks and was at a loss as to what I could do to correct the situation.

After graduation, I went home for the summer, then made my way across the United States by bus. My journey took me to Winston-Salem where I spent some time with friends then boarded the Greyhound bus to go to Boston. Sitting outside the terminal holding a ticket to Boston was a black man about my age. I asked him where he was going. He said to Andover Newton Theological School.

When we boarded the bus he went to the rear seat and didn't sit next to me. I couldn't understand why. Once in Boston, we took the same cab to the seminary. Henry Lewis became one of my close friends. We slept in the same dormitory, we studied together, we went to the movies together, we worked together, and we laughed together.

I didn't question my racial attitudes until the day when I was eating an apple and I wondered if I wanted Henry to take a bite of it. Somehow his blackness and sanitation got mixed up. I gave him a bite of my apple.

Seminary days were days when Martin Luther King Jr., was beginning his rise. There were sit-ins, arrests, and struggling for racial justice. I didn't know what to make of it. Being politically ignorant, not having faced this "race thing" before, I was astounded by it all.

As graduation neared I wondered why I couldn't seem to land a job. I had interviews with many state church executives, I had written letters to all the state secretaries in all the Western states, but I never received answers. It was mid-April and still I had not heard from anyone. Finally the First Baptist Church in Beverly, Massachusetts, called me as Associate Pastor. Later in my ministry I discovered that the reason I had difficulty being placed was first, I was Japanese, second, I was a graduate of Andover Newton. I graduated from seminary and went to work in Beverly.

In Beverly, a suburb of Boston and a lily-white community, I met with very little resistance because of my race. In fact I was like a celebrity. People used to ask, "Can you surf?" "Can you speak Japanese?" "Do you do the hula?" I didn't enjoy hearing these questions but I learned to put up with them.

Dating was still a problem because in addition to feeling inferior, I had been reared with the idea that it was wrong to marry outside of my race. Also I didn't want to be rejected by a white woman. Then I met a young woman from New Brunswick, Canada. We dated secretly for over a year before we announced our engagement. The Senior with whom I worked thought that I could do better and tried to discourage us from being married. Sandra's mother and father protested violently and would not come to the wedding. My mother and father gave grudging approval but my mother's objection centered around the issue that Sandra did not have a college education.

We got married without parental permission. I was twenty-six and Sandra twenty. My in-laws almost disowned Sandra. My parents were 5000 miles away and it didn't seem to matter. The tensions of miscegenation would not come until later.

There was little cultural adjustment for Sandra and me to make as I had so fully acculturated. Significantly too our marriage was the point at which my self-image began to improve. I began to accept myself as Japanese and to look at myself as being someone worthwhile.

We encountered very little hostility from our marriage in the churches we served. There were some eyebrows raised, but no out and out hostility.

When our first child Peter was born, my mother came to help. There was some tension between Sandra and my mother. I'm not sure that it was because of race, or because Sandra was the woman who took away from her the oldest son. But tension there was.

The births of our sons Peter and Scott helped my self-image. They were beautiful children. We wanted them to benefit from the richness of our heritages. We vowed that we would do all we could to help them to develop healthy self-images and to keep them away as much as possible from suffering a negative self-image. Their birth kindled my desire to know more about my heritage and about being Japanese.

As I formed my identity as Japanese, there was some tension, specifically over food. In 1967 when we made our first trip to Hawaii and Sandra refused to eat some of the food, there was tension!

In 1964 I went from Beverly, Massachusetts, to my own pastorate in West Acton, another suburb of Boston. This is when I began to politicize and work for racial justice. In this upper middle class white suburban town, a "yellow boy" had come to minister. These were the years of the Washington marches and the Selma demonstrations.

When asked to go on one of the marches, I wanted to go, but decided against it because this was my first year in that parish and I needed to develop relationships. Also if all the pastors in Acton went, then who would be left at home to dialogue with lay people? I stayed and preached on the race issue and then dialogued with the lay people.

The Black Power movement had a great effect on me. Even though I did it laughingly I could speak of "yellow power." In working with black people I was finding my own identity. I began to see consciously the impact racism had on me.

While working in the local church and in a suburban town, I was also working for justice on the denominational scene. I thought that I who was neither black nor white could mediate between the two.

Though there were some gains, I was pretty discouraged by the local church. So I left the parish ministry with the feeling that if white racism was to be eliminated, then white people had to do the job themselves.

The gains we made came hard and took a long time. There were people hurt by them and relationships were strained. I submitted my resignation and took a job with the denomination.

The religious bureaucracy was so busy trying to save itself when I went to work for them that it could not spend time or money in working for justice, peace, or equality in our nation. After several tries at bringing the issues to the administration of the Board of Education, and being verbally bludgeoned by them, I said, "forget it." I began to look for other opportunities for ministry.

The Office of Civil Rights of Health Education and Welfare Department offered me a job as a Civil Rights Specialist beginning at $15,400.00 assuring me of a promotion within a year and a salary of $17,200.00. It was hard to pass up. At the same time, an offer came from Evergreen Baptist Church in Los Angeles offering 50% less in salary but ministry with a Japanese-American congregation.

We struggled with the decision. I had been working with the blacks while in the local church, and while with the denomination I had worked on behalf of the browns. I decided it was time to work with my own people. That coupled with a desire to go to school led us to accepting the call to Evergreen.

The experience of the Japanese-American in Southern California is different from that of the Japanese-American in Hawaii. In Hawaii the Japanese-American is part of the majority and therefore has a majority attitude. Also though prejudice exists in Hawaii, one of the premises upon which Hawaii is built is interracial harmony so the feeling toward races is quite different.

The Southern California Japanese-American shows scars of having been hurt and oppressed. Though they have risen to become the model minority in America, they still exhibit characteristics of being oppressed. They have negative feelings about themselves, they do not think they socialize or verbalize as well as the *Hakujins* (Caucasians). They carry the hatred of the Mexicans who took away their homes while away in relocation camps. They do not trust whites. They live in fear that if they as a group did something wrong that they will be relocated.

The Japanese American church in Southern California is an enclave where they come to gain self-affirmation and to feel community. The church is the extended family for the Japanese American Christian. The ethnic church is a phenomenon of a racist society and religion.

It has been good for our family to live in a multi-cultural setting. The impact of living in a predominantly white society back East had given our oldest son a negative self image. Coming to Southern California where there are children like him, has already made a difference in his feelings about himself. He is now able to affirm himself as a Japanese.

My wife has found acceptance too. While there were problems with cultural habits, mainly food, she eats it and enjoys it and even cooks it!

As a pastor I see one of my major tasks as enabling people in the Japanese American community to affirm themselves as children of God, to see that the Gospel has relevance for all of life and to live responsibly in the world.

I look forward to a future society in which all people will be able to live as brothers and sisters working, playing, worshipping, enjoying all the benefits of God's world equally.

(Dr. David Y. Hirano graduated from Wake Forest College, Andover Newton Theological School, and the School of Theology at Claremont. He is now the pastor at Nuuanu Congregational Church in Honolulu, Hawaii.)

STORMY ROAD FOR THIS PILGRIM

Chapter I

Who Am I?

Perhaps the greatest task for any individual is to discover *who he is* in relation to others and to life in general. One cannot possess a sense of inner tranquility
without knowing who he is—and feeling good about it.
This task of discovery is a growing process of achieve-
ment; it doesn't come abruptly in all of its fulness and
clarity. Time, experience, reflection, and divine revelation are necessary for self-understanding and a healthy
sense of self-awareness.

The Dilemma of Being Obviously Ethnic

I'm an American. I'm a natural-born citizen of the
United States—and I'm proud of it. How proud am I?
As proud as any individual would be who understands
the immense freedoms and opportunities this country
provides. I'm deeply humbled before God who by divine
design has allowed *me* to be born into a land which
affords manifold potential. In capturing the exuberance
of the psalmist, I can heartily exclaim: "Praise the Lord!
Yes, really praise him! I will praise him as long as I live,
yes, even with my dying breath" (Psalm 146:1–2, *The
Living Bible*). I'm an American!

1

Yet, even though I *feel* and *think* American, I'm not looked upon as a "full-blooded, one-hundred-percent" American by many. The reason is simple—I'm of Oriental descent. Orientals just look different from Occidentals. I'm "obviously" ethnic, and all spheres of American society have not yet achieved that transcendent unity in which ethnic minorities are conceived and accepted as equal to the predominant Caucasian majority in human worth, dignity, and treatment.

Before any misconception arises let me clarify a point: I rejoice in my Japanese-American heritage. I take pride in being of Japanese ancestry. When I was a young child I thought: *What would it be like to be a Caucasian American?* I think imaginative thoughts like these are natural. I have even thought at times, *What would it be like to be a black . . . a Mexican-American . . . ?* But I have never had (nor do I now) a *sincere desire* to forsake my ancestry in exchange for another. I have too much love and respect for myself and for my parents to do so.

I'm equally proud of my *national* identity as I am of my ethnic identity. It disturbs me when people ask, "What nationality are you?" People who ask this question mean one of two things. They may falsely presume that I'm a foreigner and their question really means, "What foreign country are you from?" Having lived in the South for several years where few Orientals live, and primarily in a few large metropolitan cities, I have discovered that people easily assume that I'm a foreigner. Only after they get to know me do they realize that I'm not from a foreign country. My nationality is American!

Let me give an illustration of the feeling of frustration which sometimes rises within me when someone asks, "What nationality are you?" Let's assume that you're a member of the First Baptist Church of Dallas, Texas. You have been a member there for a great many years. You have been an active participant in the life of the church. Your commitment, loyalty, pride, and your

2

deep sense of identity is with this congregation of believers and what it represents. Now, how would you feel if other members of this same congregation repeatedly ask you, "What church do you belong to?" Their implication is, "You're a stranger here, aren't you?" Boy!

Others who ask the question, "What's your nationality?" don't mean what they are in fact saying. What they really intend to say is, "Of what ancestry are you?" or "To what American ethnic group do you belong?" They misuse the word nationality. Because of a confusion in their minds regarding the word "nationality," they abuse the use of it. But *why* do so many Americans misuse the word "nationality"?

I think we all agree it is a careless mistake. In my opinion it's an easy one to make, for since the majority of the American people are of European origin Asian-Americans are frequently conceived as "different," "foreign," or at least "not all-American." Most Americans have been taught since childhood that Asians didn't discover and build America—Europeans did. Their understanding is that Asians came later, contributed relatively little to American history, and thus the Orientals are not—they cannot be—the "real Americans." It's evident how easy it is to misuse the word "nationality" to mean *only* a certain select company of people—American whites.

Thousands of Asian-Americans such as myself are caught in this dilemma. The situation is different in the state of Hawaii, but for those living in the continental United States the problem is accentuated. Those of us who have been born and raised in this country are "red-blooded" Americans, as "red-blooded" as anyone can be. And yet ethnic minorities are often treated as though they have "foreign blood" in them and are therefore not pure Americans.

A friend of mine, who is a Japanese-American

native of Hawaii, went to a Baptist college in Arkansas and experienced this dilemma. He was born and brought up all his life in the American culture, and yet while in Arkansas he was frequently received as a foreigner. He "looked" foreign.

Although this dilemma has definitely affected and amplified *our awareness* (the Asian-American's) of physical differences, Oriental Americans as a general rule are learning to accept their "uniqueness" in good stride. But I believe that the moment others become acquainted with us we are considered and accepted as Americans in our own right. Unfortunately there are those who continue to find this "attitudinal view" difficult to accept, even if they know better. I have read and heard a statement like: "A Jap's a Jap." It is as if being Japanese is a disease and that being an American of Japanese ancestry makes no difference.

It's my conviction that Asian-Americans who have experienced the grace of God through Jesus Christ need not lament in the sense of the psalmist when he bewailed, "How shall we sing the Lord's song in a strange land" (Psalm 137:4, KJV)? To Christians of Oriental lineage who have been born and raised in the United States, America is not a "strange land." America is home. It is the nation we love. It is the only land we know and with which we can truly identify. Over the years we have left our unmistakable imprints in American heritage and culture and we continue to do so. Although only a small part, *we are a part of America*—we are what makes America *America.*

Although our dilemma may still exist in lesser or greater degrees throughout the country, there appears to be glimmering signs of a brighter tomorrow. With the increasing ease of communication and travel the world is rapidly being transformed into a "familiar community." Generally speaking, American young people today are more knowledgeable than previous generations about the hurts and struggles of the varying ethnic groups in America. In fact, it seems the whole American populace have now a sharper sensitivity toward minorities. They are more aware of the pains and injustices imposed upon ethnics and are voicing stronger disapproval for discriminating situations. There appears to be greater understanding and acceptance of Oriental-Americans today than there were twenty or thirty years ago.

It's true the American amalgamation of races has not been an altogether euphonious process, but ethnics are here to stay in this country nevertheless. This right to remain and live in this great land is not only our constitutional birthright but also our moral birthright. Racial or ethnic relations in America may not be near what it should be, but when there is an increasing understanding and acceptance for one another among *all* Americans, hope lingers on the distant horizon.

Struggling For Identity

What is my identity? In what do I desire to identify? These are difficult questions to answer. But they are vital ones; they are fundmamental and hit the roots of human existence. The first question must be inspected and answered from two points of view. The second question is directly related to the first.

What is my identity? This question can be answered from two perspectives: from the perspective of others and from my own perspective.

When others see me walking down the street, what immediately arises in their mind concerning my identity? In all probability their immediate mental response is not "John Smith, all-American" but "Oriental" or "Asian," or perhaps, "alien." People may have a hunch that I'm an American but their instantaneous response is "Oriental." My identity, then, as perceived by others is not immediately clear or apparent. That is, I could be a foreigner or an American citizen. In other words, because of my obvious ethnic appearance, people readily assign to me a *racial* identity.

In answering the above questions from *my* perspective, however, I wish to be considered (and I wish others would, too) an American first and an Oriental second. As I have lived in American society my daily consciousness confirms that I'm an American. I like pizza, football, popcorn, and frisbee.

But at times I have mixed emotions as to what actually *is* the case. For you see, I've been made conscious of my "Orientalness" to such a degree that on occassion my principal conception of myself is indeed racial . . . *Oriental.* That is, my self-awareness may be forcefully influenced by *my belief* in how others see me. Depending on my mood, I find myself fluctuating between annoyance and humor whenever someone comments with obvious surprise, "You speak good English!"

Now, in what do I desire to identify? As stated earlier, this question is directly related to the first. I want to be identified with my nationality (American) more so than my ethnic or racial identity. I am a third-generation American (Japanese *sansei*). My grandfather immigrated to Hawaii from Japan. My father was born in Hawaii, which makes him a natural-born citizen of this country since all those born in United States territorial possessions (which Hawaii was at the time) are considered so. My mother was born in Japan but came to the United States after her marriage to my father. She is now a naturalized citizen. It's easy to see, then, that I have inherited to a degree something of the culture, tastes, and philosophical outlook of the Japanese people.

So I consider myself fortunate. I'm an enriched person because of my "double" identity. My children and future grandchildren will not be quite so enriched as I in this sense because by then (if they remain in the United States) the ethnic-psychosocial identity will probably disintegrate somewhat. For example, those of you whose family history goes back many generations in this country have lost your "other" or "former" (Polish, Greek, Danish . . . ?) identity due to intermarriage and the passing of time.

This "dual" identity awareness must be interpreted in light of an earlier statement—that America is the only country I know and with which I can truly identify. This truth became a sharp reality to me when I made a trip to Japan a few years ago. For although I am of Japanese ancestry I really felt like a foreigner in the Far East! I couldn't speak the language, nor could I identify with many of the habits and emotional expressions (humor, etc.) of the Japanese people. Their way of life is with a distinctive character. Only in a limited sense could I identify with the Japanese character and cultural uniqueness. So, while I have a double identity, my experience and sympathies are first and foremost—*American.*

As a young child I recall that it was customary for my mother, after purchasing a sack of rice, to empty it in a large can container and seal it tightly in order to keep the rice conveniently stored and protected for long periods of time. As she poured the cloth sack of rice into the can, she would stop whenever her perceptive eyes fell upon a black- or brown-colored grain of rice. She would then carefully pluck it out from the rising mound of white rice and throw it away. These "off-color" grains of rice were quite easy to spot because the overwhelming majority were white. Let's use our imagination for a moment. If these "off-color" grains of rice had *feelings,* they would no doubt be insulted to be looked upon as "odd," "different," "unlikeable," or "unusable." After all, they *are* grains of rice just like their white brothers, aren't they?! This illustration reveals my feelings in the grinding struggle for identity and acceptance.

Everyone longs for acceptance. No one likes to be

considered an "oddball." My longing to be appreciated as a genuine American is rooted in my feelings of insecurity—and I think if we're honest every one of us has to a degree a sense of insecurity. I react with a quiet anger and repulsion at being looked upon as "foreign," "inferior," or "subhuman," which are the types of attitudes many Americans have for Orientals.

There is a story of a young lady who, having lost her husband who was of another nationality, longed to return with her mother-in-law to the land and people of her husband. She realized she would be a foreigner in this new land—a land which she had never lived in before. But she begged in earnest for her mother-in-law to allow her to accompany her to this new country. Her heart longing for a sense of and a ground for identity, the young woman movingly unveiled her deep affections: ". . . your people shall be my people, and your God shall be my God" (Ruth 1:16, *The Living Bible*). I'm able to understand a measure of her passions.

Search For Freedom

Because of the necessity to put into written form this inner struggle for a comfortable sense of identity, I may have given the impression that it's an overwhelming problem. It's true that the problem is a prickly reality. But in the search for release from the burden of the anxiety, a startling revelation dawned upon me.

I became a Christian at the age of thirteen. Since then the Lord has been consistently helping me to be free from this nagging need for a satisfying feeling of identity. He has led me to accept and live with my ethnic identity. And strangely, he has done so not by directly working at my knotty racial-nationality perplexity but by guiding me to find my *identity in Christ*. What a cataclysmic discovery it was for my life—what a revolutionary *technique*, if you will!

Can God answer my quest for a satisfying sense of ethnic identity by first pointing to and clarifying my identity in Christ Jesus? And can he help me to cope with ethnic stress in daily living? I think so. Perhaps God doesn't want nor does he intend for me to be too concerned about my ethnicity. Is God saying that my crisis in self-identity can be greatly abated by focusing attention to my spiritual identity? These are bold suggestions.

In the ultimate sense I am not a Japanese or a Greek or a Spaniard but a man—a man who can't find rest until he has found his rest in God (thanks, St. Augustine). I believe God has been girding me to be free from an ethnic identity hangup. He has been guiding me to be liberated from an intense desire for acceptance as a full-blooded American by first stimulating me to become a *full-blooded Christian.* In finding my identity as a child of God, I am then at liberty to accept myself and all that implies. And that implies a lot.

What do I mean by "full-blooded" Christian? Although the term itself is not a biblical one, the concept is. Jesus best explains the idea with the following instruction to his disciples:

> You cannot serve two masters: God and money. For you will hate one and love the other, or else the other way around.
>
> So my counsel is: Don't worry about things—food, drink, and clothes. For you already have life and a body—and they are far more important than what to eat and wear. Look at the birds! They don't worry about what to eat—they don't need to sow or reap or store up food—for your heavenly Father feeds them. And you are far more valuable to him than they are. Will all your worries add a single moment to your life?
>
> And why worry about your clothes? Look at the field lilies! They don't worry about theirs. Yet

9

King Solomon in all his glory was not clothed as beautifully as they. And if God cares so wonderfully for flowers that are here today and gone tomorrow, won't he more surely care for you, O men of little faith?

So don't worry at all about having enough food and clothing. Why be like the heathen? For they take pride in all these things and are deeply concerned about them. But your heavenly Father already knows perfectly well that you need them, and he will give them to you if you give him first place in your life and live as he wants you to.

So don't be anxious about tomorrow. God will take care of your tomorrow too. Live one day at a time (Matthew 6:24–34, *The Living Bible*).

Live one day at a time! If I am totally yielded to God's Lordship in my life, he will take care of all my problems and needs. He can set me free from nagging insecurities that retard any pursuit to the spirit-filled life.

The oft-asked question: "What is there to fear but fear itself?" carries a lot of truth—more truth than we often like to admit. I need not allow the thoughts and feelings of others to overwhelm me and my feelings. I can now be true to my essential nature—my *birthright* in Christ Jesus. In doing so I learn to accept and cherish myself as an indivdual of immense worth. It's as if the Holy Spirit of God is shouting deep within me: "Nelson, I have recreated your identity. You are no longer of the world, even though you are in the world. You are now mine! So just be who you are! Allow me to take my natural, all-inclusive place in your life. When you do this your hangups will inhibit you no more." Of course the journey into spiritual growth is never fast or easy. But having God beside me is more than half the battle, believe me.

I led a Bible-study group the other night. There

were thirteen of us. All were university students of varying racial identities. I had a lot to make up for. You see, the previous week I did a lousy job in the Bible-study group. I was nervous. And since I was new I wanted so much to be accepted by these students. I was so anxious that I failed to ask God and trust him to lead me through the study. Perhaps I was more worried about how the students thought of me than I was about sharing Christ's marvelous teaching with them. But the following week was different. I asked God to be at my side, to be in control. He gave me a sense of peace and calmness. Released from anxiety, I was therefore able to speak with more integrity and warmth. It really showed. During the middle of the hour-long session I consciously felt the divine presence. And God knew that I knew of his amazing grace.

In Matthew 6, Jesus repeatedly accentuates: "Take no thought for your life what you shall eat, etc." I think Jesus meant not only the material—food, shelter, clothing—but also one's concern for identity and feelings of insecurity. The message to me is: "I shouldn't let anything be of *undue* concern to me. God will somehow take care of things." And he has.

No, I'm not perfect. I haven't arrived unto that level of spiritual maturation where Christ has established his complete Lordship over me. Has anyone? Isn't this the ultimate Christian goal? To me, the Lordship of Christ is the incorporation of the spirit of the following words of Jesus into the common life of every believer:

> Jesus replied, " 'Love the Lord your God with all your heart, soul, and mind.' This is the first and greatest commandment. The second most important is similar: 'Love your neighbor as much as you love yourself.' All the other commandments and all the demands of the prophets stem from these two laws and are fulfilled if you obey them. Keep only these

11

and you will find that you are obeying all the others" (Matthew 22:37-40, *The Living Bible*).

God through Jesus Christ is the key to setting me free from ethnic stress. The solution rests ultimately in my relationship to him who has made me in his image and likeness. In accepting him and his love, I can accept myself—and not only accept but love my *own unique self.*

Chapter II

Victory in Christ

"Victory in Christ" rings like an appropriate chant for Christians who have experienced their strength as well as their salvation in the power of the Lord. But many people regard the phrase as a mere cliché, and like most clichés much of its meaning and dynamism is therefore anesthetized. Yet the truth behind these words refuse to become a paralytic victim. It is brought back to life again and again only as Christians demonstrate its truth.

Release From Anxiety

Webster defines "anxiety" as: "a state of being anxious or of experiencing a strong or dominating blend of uncertainty, agitation, or dread, and brooding fear about some contingency: uneasiness." Perhaps the word "uneasiness" is descriptive of the emotion that arises within me as a result of ethnic stress.

I was born on the "Big Island" of the state of Hawaii and raised in a tiny community approximately twelve miles from the city of Hilo. Because the "village" I lived in was too small to have a school of its own, all the children went to an elementary school in a town called Honomu, just a little ways down the mountain-side. As is true for much of Hawaii, the American white child in this area was in the minority. Consequently I don't recall any anxiety or uneasiness about my Japanese ancestral background at this early time in life. Almost all my friends were of Japanese ancestry.

When I was almost the age of nine, however, my family moved to Los Angeles, California, and my accustomed environmental "scenery" abruptly changed. It was my first taste of cultural shock! I readily recognized that in Los Angeles I was in a racial minority, that I was different in appearance from most of my new classmates. Hence the beginnings of an ethnic anxiety emerged. The pressure was on—to make new friends, to adjust to a new cultural environment, to feel accepted.

But the stress that rumbled within me was rather mild at first. For one reason, at the age of nine, children are not particularly conscious or concerned about race differences along with their underlying tensions—at least not in the same sense as are adults. For another, the east side of Los Angeles, the neighborhood to which we moved, was inhabited predominantly by Mexican-Americans. The remainder were of Asian or Caucasian lineage, with only a few blacks. So I was in school with children who were in the most part from ethnic minority groups. I felt comfortable as I identified to a degree with the "status" of the Mexican-Americans—even though I knew I was of a different ethnic family.

After five years my family moved to the city of Torrance, a suburb of Los Angeles. Again the "scenery" changed to something I had never experienced before. In the Torrance high school I attended about 97 percent (at that time) of the students were Anglo-Americans—quite a contrast from the predominately Mexican-American culture I'had left. The other students were of Latin origin with only a smattering of Orientals (there were no blacks in our high school at the time). With almost all of the 2,500 students white, I had some emotional adjustments to make.

Being a teenager now and having entered this new neighborhood in Torrance, I was made more acutely aware of my ethnic appearance. I abruptly realized I was a *Japanese*-American. It was here that my anxiety, my uneasiness about my "Orientalness," began to blossom. This self-consciousness intensified greatly . . . leading to an unhealthy emotional state.

As a youngster I was very timid, and this character trait prevailed throughout high school. Perhaps it was because my father was strict with me. But also I think my timidity was partly the result of the emergence of a feeling of insecurity—stemming largely from a subtle sense of uncomfortableness about my ethnicity. I yearned to be accepted and liked for who I was, a human being, an American, to belong and to be a part of something . . . anything.

In high school I began to associate with several fellows who became my very closest friends. It was difficult for me to enter the "inner circles" of other groups and cliques on campus. I had my share of friends. But unfortunately my ethnic self-consciousness and the resultant inferiority-insecurity complex cooled my natural desire for a wider circle of friendships. The fear of unacceptance or rebuke dictated my life. I was a slave to fear. I lacked confidence . . . and it disgusted me.

In speaking about high school, I must add the topic of girls. After all, isn't it in high school that most boys begin to take a very keen interest in young ladies? I did. But what was my relationship with girls like? Almost nil. I can count the number of times I had dated girls with one thumb! I liked girls, don't get me wrong, but I was literally afraid of them. I didn't have the foggiest idea how to communicate with them. The apprehension and stress I felt in trying to build relationships with girls were truly herculean. I may chuckle now, but it was no laughing matter then—believe me.

Consider for a moment how hard it would be for a young teenager who lived in a neighborhood in which he was of a *very* minority group, who was already painfully shy and reserved, to relate to and hopefully date a girl, any girl. This difficulty looms true for two reasons. First, to find a girl of my own ethnic identity whom I liked enough to ask for a date was like looking for a copper penny in a large barrel full of dirt. In the second place, think of the anxiety a person like myself would feel talking to, much less dating, a Caucasian girl. Not me, brother!

I remember a Japanese-American girl in high school who was especially pretty. I admired her because she had personality and charm. What normal guy wouldn't take a second look at her? Yet I recall being too scared to develop any kind of prolonged conversation with her. I'd pass her in the hall and say "hi" or I'd just smile. I couldn't get myself to do any more. I tried but I couldn't.

I have to admit that this girl's personality was just the opposite from mine. She was popular, outgoing, and friendly. Maybe that's why I was attracted to her. Interestingly, her popularity was strictly with the Caucasian girls and boys. There were a small number of other Oriental girls in our high school, but she didn't appear to be too friendly with any of them. She talked to the other Japanese girls, but she came to life around the others.

I wonder if she had inner stresses of her own? Did she go out of her way to be with Caucasian girls and boys in order to "cover up" her insecure feelings about her ethnic identity? Did she refuse close ties with other Japanese-American girls because, if she did, it may give others the impression that "Oriental girls stick together because they are one of a kind"? If I had tried to establish a meaningful relationship with her would she resist my approaches because of her insecure need to identify with and be accepted by her Anglo classmates? I don't know the answers to these questions, and I may very well be way off base with my implications. I simply bring to the surface these thoughts because they may reveal a part and parcel of the dynamic tensions within ethnic minorities who may be in a similar context.

Is there release from ethnic anxieties? According to *Roget's Thesaurus,* synonymous with "release" are "loose" or "liberate." Thus the question is raised: Is there any liberation from ethnic stress? If so, how can I be free from it? And if I have achieved release, to *what extent* have I?

It is my experience that there *can* be release from anxieties. One can find help in resolving inner conflicts and stresses in several ways. I'm not so naive as to deny the values of therapeutic counseling by trained specialists. Nor do I discount the fact that a degree of psychological/emotional help can come through the benefits of certain non-Christian religions, lay "self-awareness" groups, or simply by talking to a close and trusted friend. Whether one's anxiety stems from insecurity or from any number of reasons, the fact is clear that anxieties can to some extent disappear from one's life.

My struggle with inner stress, however, is rooted in the Christian faith. I believe in the transforming power of God. I am convinced of the changing grace of Jesus Christ. I have experienced the therapeutic work of the Holy Spirit. I have seen my life changed (ing) and transformed (ing) since my conversion experience over a decade ago. I can testify to God's miraculous power in altering attitudes, sense of values, priorities, and life's goals in many personal acquaintances. I know about the healing work of God in family life and in group life. This one thing I'm sure—God is alive and well. Those who have eyes to see, *see*.

Yes, we must be grateful for sincere and dedicated

psychologists, psychiatrists, and psychiatric social workers. They are clearly needed to perform vital services to people. Yet I'm astounded at the limitations of human help. In so many instances, all of man's genius, creativity, and good intentions fall far short of desired ends.

A heroin drug addict who has tried psychiatric therapy and all the techniques devised by man to rid him of his addiction may discover a need for help on a different dimension. His therapy from secular science may have been incomplete or unsatisfactory. I believe God can help him . . . even cure him.

A young teenage girl under tremendous emotional distress because of her recently discovered pregnancy needs immediate guidance and love. Sure, she can find help in several places. But the help that comes from God goes *beyond* human help. The realization that God accepts her for *who* she is, *as* she is, is basic to a meaningful recovery. It leads immediately to a degree of relief and inner peace. The wisdom that comes from God to "think through" her trying circumstance and make sound decisions toward an adequate solution of her trouble is indispensable. The assurance of God's vital presence instills her with courage and a steady sense of optimism in her time of dismal sensitivities. As she discovers an inner, dynamic strength undergirded by the power and intimacy of God himself, she can now better cope with the realities of her difficulties—and in the end, profit from the total experience.

An elderly man suffering from the haunting pangs of loneliness may cast away suicidal desires if he learns to accept and love himself, and thus discover a fresh dimension in his hollow existence. This God can do! This God has done for many.

The marvelous news about God's help is that it is *free to all*. It is available twenty-four hours a day, *every day*—yes, even on holidays and weekends! It is also available *everywhere*, wherever you may be.

Now that's not true with professional counselors and helping agencies. Their help may not be free at all. It's often not available twenty-four hours a day, every day. And it's not available everywhere you happen to be. It has extreme difficulty reaching man's spiritual nature. Man's help has severe limitations. God's love, on the other hand, transcends time, space, and any impossible situation. The love of God meets a man where he hurts. The Holy Spirit of God can penetrate the hardness of a man's heart and do things that baffle the minds of the scientific age.

Should one use human help? Sure. When in trouble, use any help available which you can afford and which you strongly feel is to your best advantage. If you believe your pastor can minister to you, talk to him. Be aware, however, that many times an unskilled minister can drop acid on the open wound of your hurt. If you can afford a competent psychologist and feel he can relate to you, go to him. Go to a relative or a trusted friend—they *may* be of more help than anyone else. But a Christian, especially one who has a vibrant faith in the living Lord, is particularly blessed because not only can he utilize man's help, he also has access to help "from above." And it is this deeper dimension in his life that often makes the difference for him.

The quality and abundance of God's help is beyond human measure. God's love for you and me is in all sense of the word *boundless.* He helps us according to his grace and his good pleasure. The psalmist declared ages ago: "For I cried to him and he answered me! He freed me from all my fears" (Psalms 34:4, *The Living Bible*).

Yes, God can loosen the shackles of burdensome ethnic anxieties, and Jesus Christ is the means by which I'm set free from the corroding chains of insecurity. The Christ who calmed the raging sea, the Mighty One who while on earth revealed divine serenity in many stressful situations, and supremely at the cross, and this Lord who epitomizes the transcendent strength and poise of God the Father, *he* has the energetic capacity to empower *me* with serene confidence. He stimulates my vision, restores my faith, and like a breath of cool air, refreshes my hope.

But if I have achieved release from ethnic stress, to what extent is this release? That's a good question. So much of the uneasiness I have felt in the past is now under control. That is, conditions which produced anxiety years ago are no longer stressful today. I'm now better able to cope with varying life experiences.

I'm not saying that I have achieved total release from ethnic tensions. I have not. At times I still get emotionally tense—when going for a job interview, speaking in a group, or visiting an all-white church for the first time. Of course, part of the stress felt during these times is natural. It happens to most people. But I do know that my ethnicity plays a significant role in the extent of my uneasiness. The degree of my self-consciousness and anxiety is not as great as it was before, but there are definitely those instances in which I do not feel comfortable or relaxed as I would like to be.

The apostle John's words really hit home to me at this point: "There is no fear in love; but perfect love casteth out fear: because fear hath torment. He that feareth is not made perfect in love" (I John 4:18, KJV). Herein lies a key to my dilemma. If "his love is perfected in us" (I John 4:12), as John says, I can eliminate all fears. Oh how relentlessly arduous is the task of allowing God's love to grow in us. But oh how relentless is that love to grow in us!

As you can see, I believe in God's absolute power to release unnecessary anxieties from me. But I'm not sure that an absolute elimination of all stress is in fact practical or good. I wonder what life would be like without some form of tension? I may have *my* tense moments at certain life circumstances, but don't *you* have those life situations in which you are anxious? It seems reasonable to conjecture that because human beings are perpetually susceptible to a myriad of stimuli, man must creatively learn to survive with various forms of stress and tension. Some forms of stress and "excitement" are healthy and an intergral part of what it means to be alive. It is when man's anxious moments appear too frequently or in a too profound degree that his inner stress may be deemed "abnormal." And regarding ethnic stress, with divine help any person is able to break the debilitating strictures of unhealthy anxieties. I know. God's been working on me for quite a while.

Perhaps the word "relief" is more descriptive of the work and accomplishment of God in dealing with my ethnic fears. That is, God helps me to find relief from ethnic tensions; but I haven't achieved complete release of these anxieties—due to a fault or lack on my part or because of an intention on God's part. Regardless, the point is that God's work in my life is a process; and within this process he is ever lifting me out of the inhibiting shackles of fear and insecurity . . . a mounting liberation from ethnic anxiety.

Necessity For Growth

Fundamental to God's working in my life is the phenomenon of growth. Growth is basic to life. When you quit growing as a person, you will begin to smell the breath of death. Growth in every human sphere is at the root of God's will for mankind. It is the interest and activity of God in my life . . . in every life.

Just as the child Jesus "grew and waxed strong in spirit" (Luke 1:80, KJV), I am to do the same and "become more and more in every way like Christ" (Ephesians 4:15, *The Living Bible*). I am to develop and mature to the point where I can truthfully boast with

21

Paul, "I have been crucified with Christ: and I myself no longer live, but Christ lives in me" (Galations 2:20, *The Living Bible*). You talk about a challenge . . . !

Books on human growth and development are abundant. Colleges offer courses in child, adolescent, and adult psychology. All social scientists agree that a human person is a growing organism. But somehow the church must convince the world of the necessity for spiritual development. For without the growth of the spiritual side of man decadence in every society will continue. The Christian says that man is more than an animal, that in reality his spiritual nature is the ultimate ground of his being.

I am having "tastes" of victory in Christ in handling ethnic anxiety because of the spiritual and moral growth taking place in my life. As I begin to peel off the psychological hangups of my old nature and allow the healing presence of the spirit of Christ in my heart, I am empowered to respond to life in a free and natural way. The simple spontaneity of living life anew each day with Christ at the helm of my consciousness and will is a delightful experience.

Growing in Christ and finding victory through him helps an individual to cope with any problem or difficulty. But the journey in spiritual development isn't always easy. As I see it, the process of growing involves several important features: (a) change, (b) adjustment, (c) risk (being vulnerable), (d) inquisitiveness, and (e) widsom. The interrelationship of all of these features in growth will quickly be seen. But for clarity I will discuss each of these characteristics separately.

Growth means *change*. This is true for physical as well as spiritual growth. Take a simple illustration. As a youngster I didn't bother shaving before going to school. I didn't need to. This morning our three-year-old son Maury slipped into his school clothes and I hurried him off to preschool. In two minutes he's dressed and ready!

But as an adult I must shave every day . . . and some day soon Maury the teenager will need to pick up the habit.

Growing means change in the spiritual dimension as well. When I was a young child I really didn't care to be thrust into the hurts and sufferings of others. I was too self-centered. Now I am significantly more interested in people and better able to empathize with their pains. I have grown. Growing in every human dimension is a very natural part of life, or at least it should be.

The telephone rang. It was for me. Who could it be? I wondered. Who would be calling me at 12:15 P.M., just a few minutes after finishing our worship service that Sunday? The mysterious caller asked for the pastor. I was summoned. The man's voice communicated hurt and fear. He very reservedly pleaded for help. His young wife and three-year-old daughter were hungry, without money, and without a place to sleep. Their story is too long and involved to relate here. In brief, I went to the hotel they were staying in, took them home with us, fed them, gave them a few useful articles, and drove them to the bus station where I purchased tickets for them to go to Arizona to stay with their relatives. Why my involvement? Because through the years God has been changing my calloused, egocentric nature . . . for times like this. To have said, "No, I don't have the time for you," would have grated against my conscience mercilessly. I have grown . . . with time . . . to love.

Growing also necessitates adequate *adjustment.* Without it growing skids to an abrupt halt. If, for example, I refuse to adjust to the whiskers growing on my face, how would you react upon seeing a mass of unkempt and tangled facial growth? Likewise, if I can't make satisfactory adjustments to the new awareness and spiritual awakenings occurring in my life, I am like a first-time swimmer—making a lot of splashes but getting nowhere.

The spiritually maturing process requires the conquering of various important stages in succession. One can't perform like the apostle Paul overnight; it is impossible to walk a mile without taking that first step. There must be adjustment at each stage of spiritual development.

When we first brought him home with us Charlie was only three months old. He was a beautiful Siamese kitten. In his own way, though, Charlie rebelled against the sudden and unkind change in his life. He was rudely separated from his protective mother and his fun-loving, romping, brothers and sisters and placed in a completely strange home. The familiar sights and smells and noise were gone. Instead he was forced to live with a young family that never owned a pet before, and knew absolutely nothing about cats, particularly Siamese. Charlie showed his fear and disapproval of his new family and home by isolating himself for days, eating and drinking little. We begged and sometimes scolded him for behaving that way. Yet beneath our outward frustrations we knew that in time, in Charlie's time, he would come around. And he did. As he began to accept a new makeshift bed, a new home with new masters, he shed some of his fear and anger. His appetite increased. He put on weight. He became more jolly and playful. We were relieved. We grew more fond of that little cat because he was beginning to respond to his surroundings. Charlie was growing! What worked for a cat can work for you.

To grow also means to be *vulnerable,* to take risks. The trouble is that so many of us are reluctant to take chances in life, to "go out on a limb." Fearful of the unknown, we exemplify pale victims of the status quo. We cherish the security of the familiar and the customary. But if you aren't willing to be vulnerable, little change (growth) will come your way. When your spirit for *adventure* wanes, the spice of life turns insipid and you no longer manifest an active, fascinating personality. The dull individual does not live in the fullest sense; he merely exists.

On the other hand, the truly growing person displays an unquenchable itch to discover all the good that life offers. He's not an intellectual or social recluse. He doesn't shy away from new ideas, new attitudes, new possibilities, new experiences, and new ways of doing things. He doesn't cling to everything new, only the new that is good and the new that is better or more complete than the old. The growing person experiments, "sticks his neck out" for a cause in which he believes until he is proven wrong. If he is wrong about something he doesn't hide in shame, for he humbly knows he is far superior to the multitude of timid souls who are sorely afraid of life—the life of risk-taking. If he is wrong about something he simply shrugs it off and says to himself that he has gained infinitely more than he has lost from the risk of involvement and inquiry. So the maturing individual is a "chancer." He knows if he is to climb the heights of intellectual, emotional, and spiritual maturity, he must set his eyes and challenge life. There is something refreshing and, yes, awesome about a person who dares to really live! He's exciting.

Tom Dempsey, the place-kicker for the Los Angeles Rams, deserves admiration. And not because I've been a staunch Ram fan for almost two decades, but because I simply marvel at the man. Look at him! He's fat, pudgy, deformed in his hand and feet. He's no Prince Charming. He looks more like the corner laundry man than a highly respected professional football player.

I often wonder what hardships Tom had to overcome to be what he is today? I believe that underneath that awkward helmet and blue-and-gold uniform is a man of a man, full of pride and determination. What kind and how much ridicule and negativism did he have to endure to persevere the waves of pessimism that must have come his way? There's no telling unless you just ask him. But I believe Tom has achieved greatness because he was willing to be vulnerable. Other's ridicule and lack of confidence did not deter his determination. A chancer? You bet.

A natural corollary to the characteristic of risk-taking in the growing individual is the feature of *inquisitiveness*. Frankly, I don't know how one goes about acquiring an inquisitive spirit. I assume everyone is born with a degree of it. But when one becomes a Christian, God begins to actively nurture this characteristic in the life of the believer. It is the spark that has led many Christian saints to greatness. Unfortunately, many of us fall short of our potential for growth because we lack this *quest to inquire*. The spirit of inquisitivenes, if not utilized daily, tends to weaken and finally fade from our personality. All progress depends on it.

I believe every invention, every creative change or reform in life is the direct result of someone's inquisitive spirit. What would the world of Christianity be like had it not been for the inquisitive nature of a Luther, Wesley, or a Carey? Life is a fascinating frontier. And there is so much yet to experience and discover! The development and enrichment of an individual and of mankind depend on an insatiable quest for the fresh, the new, the good, and the better. God desires every individual to live a more abundant life. But the one who does so is the one who is inquisitive—he "seeks" and he "knocks" . . . into every dimension of life. And more often than not, he finds.

Finally, the growing process requires *wisdom*. Not mere knowledge, but skillful perceptivity. According to Webster's, wisdom means the "ability to discern inner qualities and relationships: . . . good sense."

The discernment of that which is good and wholesome, the healthy sense to reject those things which are detrimental to physical, mental, and spiritual vigor, the ability to perceive one's aptitudes and strengths as well

26

as one's weaknesses, and the commitment to strive to enlarge his potential—for his sake and for the sake of mankind—this is wisdom.

The author of Proverbs 4:5–9 (*The Living Bible*) urges men to passionately cherish it:

> ". . . Learn to be wise," he said, "and develop good judgment and common sense! I cannot overemphasize this point." Cling to wisdom—she will protect you. Love her—she will guard you.
>
> Determination to be wise is the first step toward becoming wise! And with your wisdom, develop common sense and good judgment. If you exalt wisdom, she will exalt you. Hold her fast and she will lead you to great honor; she will place a beautiful crown upon your head.

The truth of the matter is that a person can value change, be vulnerable in taking risks, and be inquisitive, but if he lacks the wisdom to choose *the good*—he may evolve into an antichrist rather than a saint! Take intelligence. An intelligent individual can be a good man or an evil man. Like a baby bird imitating its mother, God's intention is for all men to grow into the image of Jesus Christ, and without wisdom this transformation is impossible. The wise man chooses God. And in God he has access to the source of infinite Wisdom. Therefore "to grow" must be qualified to mean "to grow in God." To fully mature is to mature as only one can who possesses a keen awareness of God's sovereignty over life.

There is a man whose image still affects me today, even after long years of separation. He gave 20 percent of his large income to the church. Why? Why when most Christians struggle to give 10 percent? I have to believe that it was because as he grew into the image of God, he became wise. For the Christian, to grow is to grow in wisdom.

As I grow with the grace of God, I am finding success in lessening the emotional and psychological stresses rooted in the insecurities of an ethnic self-consciousness. Praise God. And although growth and change at times come slowly, I find deep comfort in these encouraging words:

> O Jacob, O Israel, how can you say that the Lord doesn't see your troubles and isn't being fair? Don't you yet understand? Don't you know by now that the everlasting God, the Creator of the farthest parts of the earth, never grows faint or weary? No one can fathom the depths of his understanding. He gives power to the tired and worn out, and strength to the weak. Even the youths shall be exhausted, and the young men will all give up. But they that wait upon the Lord shall renew their strength. They shall mount up with wings like eagles; they shall run and not be weary; they shall walk and not faint (Isaiah 40:27-31, *The Living Bible*).

God continues to be aware of my inner battles. His awareness, though, is not one characterized by inertia but by activity. And as long as he is active in my life, I am growing.

Chapter III

A Challenge to Ethnic Minority Christians

I write this chapter specifically for ethnic minority Christians. I believe ethnic minority Christians need encouragement. For although they are Christians, the biting reality remains that they are still ethnic minorities, people who continue to contest for equality in all phases of American society.

My dream is for Anglo-Americans and every American ethnic minority—Jew, Chinese, Indian, Japanese, Samoan, black, whatever—to create an attitude of mind and heart that accepts everyone as equally worthy of kind and honest treatment. The fulfillment of that dream is far from us.

Yet this country is seeing striking improvements in social justice. Laws are changing. But laws and societal restructuring represent mere surface modifications. Many living in American society are experiencing no great transformation of racial attitudes. It's easier to melt steel than it is to soften the rigid sinews of a warped heart. Because of slow-changing racial attitudes, then, I feel ethnic minority Christians must be encouraged to understand their spiritual identity in Christ Jesus. In doing so they can meet the relentless challenges of ethnic stress with cool heads—and with heads held high.

Accept Christ's Love For You

There is a great need for ethnic American Christians to voice a reaffirmation of their sacred value to themselves and to God. We are worthy of God's love, not because we merit or deserve divine love, but because it is God's generous gift to us: "For God so loved the world that he gave his only begotten Son" (John 3:16, KJV). God gave to all men his Son Jesus Christ as an embracing demonstration of his kinetic love for all mankind.

Giving here does not necessitate nor does it imply merit on man's part. God gave because he loved—that was it. This simple fact is beyond human comprehension. Anyone who claims to understand the mystery of divine love speaks with deceiving lips. Paul affirms the incomprehensibility of God's love when he declares, "the love of God, which passeth knowledge" (Eph. 4:19, KJV). I want to urge Christians of ethnic lineage to *fully* accept God's love—it is his free gift to you.

Many years ago when I was eight years old, my family was on the verge of moving from Hawaii to California. My Hawaiian grandparents were naturally not overjoyed with the decision but wished us well. One day very near to the time when we were to board the plane leaving the beautiful islands, my grandfather took out an elegantly designed pocket knife, one which contained all sorts of blades. He knew I wanted the knife badly, after all he was a young boy once. I knew it was his prized knife, and I never dreamed he would give it to me. But as a jesture of affection and remembrance he offered me that ornate black knife. I really couldn't believe it! I didn't work for it or deserved it in any way. Grandpa just gave it to me as a token of his love, and I simply accepted it. God's love is like that—and we must respond to him in similar fashion.

Let me amplify the above truth from the Bible. One

30

day as Jesus sat at Jacob's well a Samaritan woman (note her ethnic identity) approached. In the course of their very interesting conversation Jesus proclaimed to the woman: "Whosoever drinketh of the water that I shall give him shall never thirst; but the water that I shall give him shall be in him a well of water springing up into everlasting life" (John 4:14, KJV). You will note that twice Jesus employed the word "give" in this verse. It's obvious that the act of giving eliminates any purchase on our part; giving only requires acceptance. We accept—approve, assent to, receive—the giving on the part of God. I don't believe any individual can ascend to the heights of a spiritual conversion experience without first recognizing the gift of God in Jesus Christ and simply and wholely embracing him. Nor do I believe a Christian can journey to a deeper spiritual maturity without always accepting the bountiful love of God expressed through his many gifts to us throughout life.

Now, the ethnic Christian must acknowledge that at Jacob's well Jesus spoke to a "despised" Samaritan, a non-Jew. This occurrence has profound implications for ethnic minorities today for it vividly displays "the breadth, and length, and depth, and height" (Eph. 3:18, KJV) of God's impartial love for all the races of man. Ethnic minorities have an equal privilege and responsibility to respond to divine love as do any man or woman in America.

I get disturbed when some imply that the blacks, Orientals, and Chicanos in the United States or the primitive natives in Africa or Asia are to be extra thankful that God loves them, too. In preaching, many pastors would proclaim or imply something abasing as this: "Yes, Christ died even for the blacks in the ghetto and the ignorant savages of tropical Brazil. How grateful these scums of the earth must be to hear that Christ (pictured as white, of course) even stooped low enough to offer *them* help!" The unfortunate occurrence of this

31

"point of view" is rooted in a combination of the superior-inferior sociological phenomenon and a fundamental misinterpretation of the Word of God. This is tragic and unfortunate.

The superior-inferior principle of life is as old as Adam. The Jews feel superior to Gentiles, the Chinese feel superior to the Russians, the Russians feel superior to the Chinese, *ad infinitum*. The superior-inferior fact of life quite easily develops in any people and is particularly difficult to erase. The fierce competition at the Olympic games testifies to the degree of pride every national competitor feels. Racial or national pride is natural, but it can so easily rise into a very vicious and imbalanced feeling of superiority. It is a danger no one is completely free from.

It's deplorable that some Christians misinterpret Scripture to the degree that they see God's love for the minorities, the poor, and the down-and-outers as a greater miracle than God's love for them. Like the Pharisees of old, these Christians seem to think that those most deserving of God's mercy are the righteous, the holy, and the respectable. Although Christians of this sort concede that Scripture reveals God's love is for all people, they erroneously imply that the disadvantaged, the lesser educated, the minorities, are to be especially thankful for God's boundless grace. Now, this attitiude is inexcusable because nowhere in Scripture do we find such a point of view! Indeed, Jesus sharply condemns such "thinking" (see Matthew 23). The New Testament asserts in clarion tones that in his dealings with men God sees no distinction in the races. Jew or non-Jew, everyone is regarded on the basis of his *humanity* and not on the basis of class, sex, or race (Galations 3:28). All are equal in that all are in need of God's redeeming love.

Accept God's love for you.

Recognize Your Uniqueness

The ethnic minority Christian is unique in three ways: (1) he is unique in his humaness; (2) he is unique in his ethnic minority status; and (3) he is unique as a Christian. In a day when some form of "uniqueness" is passionately sought by so many, ethnic minority Christians can cherish their form of singularity! The quality of uniqueness carries the drawing power of attention to itself. Ethnic Christians must recognize their uniqueness and reap its fruitful advantages.

First, the ethnic minority is unique as a human being. Every individual is distinct, totally "other" in his relation to others. Since no two persons are alike, the ethnic minority can relish his unique individuality. He can take pride in his "specialness," as can any human being. I guess this is the way God created his universe. Every snowflake is different. Every stone and tree, if one looks close enough, have a multitude of distinct variations. It is the wonder of divine genius that every human life that breathes "stands alone," a creature specially formed for a specially unique existence.

The ethnic minority Christian is also unique in his link to American society. He is a racial minority, and therefore frequently a victim of prejudice. Although many regard ethnic minorities with sorrow or uneasiness, they are people who possess certain advantages. May I suggest a few?

First of all, he sprinkles variety and interest in American life. Consider San Francisco. The city would be rather bland indeed without the exotic features of Chinatown and the conspicuous Oriental population. New Orleans would not be New Orleans without the aura of its rich history and the contributions of its resilient blacks. New York City would not be an intriguing metropolis without the phemomenal mixture of Puerto

Ricans, Jews, Orientals, etc. The 1974 baseball champion Oakland Athletics would not have been quite so charismatic a team without the talents and personalities of Bert Campaneris, Reggie Jackson, and Vida Blue. The character, the atmosphere, the peculiarity, and yes, the soul of countless organizations, institutions, and even churches would be drastically altered without the stimulating presence and influence of ethnic minorities. He who brings such potency and casts such a spell is in a delightful position, is he not?

Secondly, ethnic minorities in America have the opportunity to help bridge the gap of misunderstanding between the peoples of the world. Too frequently anger, resentment, and distrust result between the United States and another country. Perhaps ethnic minorities can in a small way help the American people to see that other races are indeed human beings, people who deserve respect and understanding.

Let me illustrate. In 1969 I was appointed a Texas Baptist Student Union summer missionary to the University of Texas, Austin. My mission was to help establish a ministry for the hundreds of international students enrolled at the school. Those students whom I befriended were from Indonesia, one from Greece, one from Peru, two from Japan. There were others, but from these relationships you can see that I had an expansion of my vision for the brotherhood of man as a result of my ties with these foreign students. I learned to love and respect them, and they, me. Building a relationship across racial and cultural barriers is slow and frustrating sometimes, but the rewards are worth their weight in gold. As an American I can no longer think of Greece in simply superficial terms. I think of Peter when I think of Greece. And although I don't recall their names, faces come to my mind as I think of Thailand and Peru and Japan.

Thirdly, the ethnic minority is often the possessor of

two worlds, of two identities. Many ethnic minorities in America retain their ancestral language, customs, and thought patterns. They understand and enjoy the numerous advantages of their racial identity as well as their identity as an American. What sensible person would not be envious of the culturally enriched individual of two worlds?

Finally, not only is the ethnic Christian unique in his humanness and in his status in American life, but he is also peculiar in his spiritual dimension. In a nation where millions are spiritual pagans, and countless millions whose names lie on the church rolls but who nevertheless live with utter disregard for God, it is rare indeed to find a person whose faith in the relevancy and sanctity of the Christian religion manifests a fresh vibrancy. An ethnic minority who is a Christian, then, can rejoice also in his spiritual, Kingdom identity—the most blessed uniqueness of all.

I cannot help but think of Anita. This Chinese young lady from Hong Kong is an example of joy and exuberance. She simply loves Jesus Christ. She always seems to wear a wide smile which I know comes from her heart. Anita certainly stands out in a world of insecurity and fear. She radiates peace. I'm sure others feel the same way about her in Fort Worth, Texas, where she is a seminarian.

Recognize your uniqueness.

Suffer With God If You Must

"Humble men are very fortunate!" he told them, "for the Kingdom of Heaven is given to them. Those who mourn are fortunate! for they shall be comforted. The meek and lowly are fortunate! for the whole wide world belongs to them.

"Happy are those who long to be just and

good, for they shall be completely satisfied. Happy are the kind and merciful, for they shall be shown mercy. Happy are those whose hearts are pure, for they shall see God. Happy are those who strive for peace—they shall be called the sons of God. Happy are those who are persecuted because they are good, for the Kingdom of Heaven is theirs.

"When you are reviled and persecuted and lied about because you are my followers—wonderful! Be happy about it! Be very glad! for a tremendous reward awaits you up in heaven. And remember, the ancient prophets were persecuted too " (Matt. 5:3;12, *The Living Bible*).

The *San Francisco Chronicle* on November 27, 1974, carried an article about an incident which depicts the sour nature of racial bigotry. According to the article, a nineteen-year-old Chinese-American sailor was accused of throwing a pie into the face of an officer who had called the young sailor a "gook." The attorney for the Chinese-American contended that if his client wasn't a member of a minority group he would not be facing a navy court-martial. The attorney declared that his client's defense would reveal that the navy maintains an institutionalized prejudice against Asian-Americans, delegating them to less prestigious jobs than Caucasians. In pretrial motions, when the defense attorney asked the presiding officer whether the term "gook" would be regarded as derogatory by most Asian-Americans, an affirmative answer was given. Regardless of the court decision reached, the undisputed fact remains that racial prejudice is a living disease within the military services; and, of course, the infection is an extension of that which is found in society.

I mention the article because it reminds us of the alarming reality of current racial tensions. But more than that, it is important for ethnic minorities to consider the idea of "suffering" in the life of the Christian believer. More than likely the Chinese-American sailor was not a Christian. But if *you* are, your reaction, your ability to cope, or your handling of a similar situation will largely depend upon your understanding of suffering in the Christian life.

Is suffering inherent in the spirit-filled life? Are Christians to endure the many forms of persecution, discrimination, and injustice? How is one to understand Proverbs 19:11: "A wise man restrains his anger and overlooks insults" (*The Living Bible*)? Are you as an ethnic minority Christian to suffer with the inequalities and subtle forms of prejudice inflicted upon you? If so, in what sense are you to?

I believe Christians should actively seek any fair and lawful means to establish justice. I believe in social action and social justice for everyone. As a Christian I'm compelled to honor the laws of the land and to respect the American system of government, however imperfect it is. Yet I believe in the need to reform unfair laws or policies which perpetuate racial discrimination, at the same time realizing that this is not enough.

But when laws change so slowly, what are Christians to do? When "incidental" discriminatory attitudes and practices occur how should an ethnic Christian behave? With anger? Revenge? Hatred? Withdrawal? Apathy? When ethnic jokes or slurs are voiced in private or public, how should you feel, think, react? How do you begin to explain it to your children? How do you help them to face their ethnicity in a society that judges you by it?

The ethnic Christian who suffers any form of indignity can find immense comfort from the great "love chapter,"(1 Corinthians 13). I don't believe one can suffer in a Christ-like spirit if the love of God is not overflowing in him. It is this bountiful love of God that powers an individual to endure his hurts. There ought to be no gulf between the realities of love and suffering. Paul very beautifully described this unity by claiming that love ("charity") is the irreplaceable root of the Christian faith. That is, Christian suffering is suffering in love. He states, "I am nothing," if he has not love. Listen to him:

Charity suffereth long, and is kind; charity envieth not; charity vaunteth not itself, is not puffed up, Doth not behave itself unseemly, seeketh not her own, is not easily provoked, thinketh no evil; Rejoiceth not in iniquity, but rejoiceth in the truth; Beareth all things, believeth all things, hopeth all things, endureth all things. Charity never faileth: (I Corinthians 13:4–8a, KJV).

Note the descriptive verbs used to color the meaning of love: "suffereth," "beareth," "believeth," "hopeth," and "endureth." Paul appears to say that the Christian should cultivate and polish these golden qualities of faith and make them an indubitable part of his character. They are the stuff out of which the glory of God shines; they are the grains of salt which proclaim the genius and resiliency of Christianity as no word can. The Christian's tragic weakness is his glaring inability to sharpen and express this "love-suffering" dynamic.

He stood out like a fresh marshmallow in a tray of charcoal. Williams was his last name. He was a preacher's kid, a tall, thin, blond-haired, red-lipped lad of ten or eleven years of age. Our elementary school in east Los Angeles was made up predominantly of Mexican-Americans. But I recall vividly how this quiet Mennonite Christian boy withstood the tease and occasional physical abuse of the others. He gained my deepest admiration, for in his own quiet way he displayed an unusual degree of poise and confidence. He never was afraid of a fight, even though his frail body could not stand up to the sturdier Mexican-American lads. Yet he

rarely fought, for he would rather endure the frequent taunts of the boys than "throw blows." His steady eyes and mannerism told me he wasn't a "chicken." Those Mexican-American boys had it all wrong—Williams was not a weakling. He was strong, courageous . . .and unusually so.

Numerous verses interspersed throughout Scripture reveal the principle of suffering as a basic trait in the committed believer. The Old Testament teaches the "suffering servant" motif. That is, the nation Israel (God's people) and the coming Messiah can be interpreted to enter the role of the suffering servant. The New Testament clearly depicts the same motif. James 5:11 (KJV) says, "We count them happy that endure." Hebrews 11:25 (KJV) states, "choosing rather to suffer affliction with the people of God." God calls his people to face persecutions by being long-suffering, enduring the miriad forms of hardships that come one's way. No, I'm not suggesting that Christians stand idly by while evil and injustice run rampant. But a Christian is asked to endure while actively working for justice, which I recognize is often slow in coming. We must suffer for Christ's sake—a task for the strong, not the weak.

Now, there is a dimension of Christian suffering that is unheralded by religious leaders. This "other" dimension proposes profound implications for the Christian. It's not something new; hardly anything I say marks a distinctly original thought. No, it's not new, but the idea must be "renewed" for it will help any of us in our walk through life's rugged road. I'm speaking about *suffering with God*.

The Old Testament abounds in the idea of the suffering God. God's suffering results from man's disobedience and sin—and man's tragic failure is exactly the cause of *His* suffering. Man's ruin affects the entire universe, and God is moved. The psalmist cries, "How often did they provoke him in the wilderness, and grieve him in the desert" (Psalm 78:40, KJV). Isaiah graphically portrays the coming Messiah as a suffering servant of God: "He is despised and rejected of men; a man of sorrows, and acquainted with grief . . . Surely he hath borne our griefs and carried our sorrows" (Isaiah 53:3–4, KJV). The Bible reveals a God who shares in the travails of his people. Just as man's heart is restless until he finds his rest in God, so God's heart is restless until he finds his place in every man.

The New Testament also exposes the same kind of God. I know of no other religion that makes such ado about a transcendent God who grieves *for* and *with* his people (the saints) and all people (nonbelievers, as Jesus weeping for the stiff-necked city of Jerusalem)—hence his open link to humanity and the world as we know it.

But perhaps the most intense biblical narration on the qualities of the suffering God lies in some celebrated words of Jesus. In Matthew 25:31–46, Jesus picturesquely describes the scene at the second coming of the Son of Man. Here we see in lucid terminology the identification of Jesus with the sufferings of the human race:

> But when I, the Messiah, shall come in my glory, and all the angels with me, then I shall sit upon my throne of glory. And all the nations shall be gathered before me. And I will separate the people as a shepherd separates the sheep from the goats, and place the sheep at my right hand, and the goats at my left.
>
> Then I, the King, shall say to those at my right, "Come, blessed of my Father, into the Kingdom prepared for you from the founding of the world. For I was hungry and you fed me; I was thirsty and you gave me water; I was a stranger and you invited me into your home; naked and you clothed me; sick and in prison, and you visited me."
>
> Then these righteous ones will reply, "Sir,

40

when did we ever see you hungry and feed you? Or thirsty and give you anything to drink? Or a stranger, and help you? Or naked, and clothe you? When did we ever see you sick or in prison and visit you?"

And I, the King, will tell them, "When you did it to these my brothers you were doing it to me!" Then I will turn to those on my left and say, "Away with you, you cursed ones, into the eternal fire prepared for the devil and his demons. For I was hungry and you wouldn't feed me; thirsty, and you wouldn't give me anything to drink; a stranger, and you refused me hospitality; naked, and you wouldn't clothe me; sick, and in prison, and you didn't visit me."

Then they will reply, "Lord, when did we ever see you hungry or thirsty or a stranger or naked or sick or in prison, and not help you?"

And I will answer, "When you refused to help the least of my brothers, you were refusing to help me."

And they shall go away into eternal punishment; but the righteous into everlasting life (*The Living Bible*).

Forasmuch then as Christ hath suffered for us in the flesh, arm youselves likewise with the same mind: (I Peter 4:1a, KJV).

Arm yourselves with the same mind. As God suffers for mankind, learn to share his sensitivities. God truly identifies in your sorrows. You are not alone. God is *with* you, may we be *with him.*

Make Each Day a New Task

If you accept Christ's love for you, if you recognize

your uniqueness as an ethnic minority Christian, and if you know that as you suffer God is "with you," then you're ready to meet the challenges of each new day with a joyful, humble confidence. For the ethnic Christian, the intricacies of life will produce those sensitive situations which will examine with cunning scrutiny his capacity for patience, love, and endurance. He must be at his best.

Jesus continues to demand of us, "Why stand ye here all the day idle?" (Matthew 20:6, KJV). To fully live is to recognize the awesome intention of God in calling his stewards to make every day a new task of personal growth and victory. The challenge of each day summons us to struggle with life, encounter its problems squarely, and allow the Holy Spirit to direct our every mental-spiritual response to these life situations.

The spirit in which life ought to be approached has been amply depicted by the psalmist: "This is the day which the Lord hath made; we will rejoice and be glad in it" (Psalm 118:24, KJV). This is to be coupled with the following counsel: "Trust in the Lord with all thine heart; and lean not unto thine own understanding. In all thy ways acknowledge him, and he shall direct thy paths" (Proverbs 3:5–6, KJV).

Make each day a new task of discovery and growth. A bright, exciting day dawns on anyone who openly accepts the challenges of life. As someone has said, love life and life will love you back. Hate it, deny it, hide from it, curse it, and it will return to you in kind.

Chapter IV

A Challenge to Anglo-American Christians

True racial harmony will not be seen in the near future.
The raging crosscurrents of strife among the various
racial segments in the country are too deeply ingrained.
But I believe that sincere Christians united, however
small their numbers, can help build healthy attitudes in
society that will begin to melt the thick wax of prejudice.
Christians of ethnic minority status can make their con-
tribution in easing the sick vibrations of racial bigotry.
But because of their sheer numbers, Anglo-American
Christians must be out in the forefront in the drama of
this battle. They are the ones entrusted with the major
responsibility for enhancing the evolution of a societal
atmosphere in which equality, justice, and respect
abound for all Americans.

How can a careful study of Scripture help the Anglo-American find a base of support from which he can
launch out to become a courageous instrument of God's
peace? Can a more defined awareness of the worth and
dignity of a human being contribute to a healthier racial
attitude?

What can you do, as a white American Christian, to
demonstrate the love and work of God in your life?

Study the Confrontation of the Early Apostles With Racial Groups

In order to calm the often damaging tides of racial turmoil, Anglo-American Christians must review the Word of God and discover how the early saints learned to cope with their own weaknesses as they intermingled with men and women of other nationalities.

The first Christians were Jews. They came from a distinct background of profound cultural and religious identity. How did they relate to other ethnic groups as they sought to diffuse the universal message of redemption? What were some of the basic teachings inherent in their faith which shaped their attitudes and guided their actions?

The first astonishing fact about the phenomenal growth of Christianity in the first century is that it was accomplished primarily by Jews. If we properly assess the Jewish thought patterns in the time of Christ we will note the utter contempt many harbored for Gentiles, those who were not of "the seed of Israel." And yet the faith in Jesus Christ spread throughout the Roman world, springing from the base of Jewish Christianity. Can anyone doubt the marvelous work of the spirit of God in human history?

By far the supreme Jewish personality who exemplified the true spirit of the Godhead was Paul. He was "the apostle to the Gentiles." If ever a man lived whom ethnic Christians can hold up in highest regard, it is this man. It was both a product of scholarly wisdom and divine inspiration that motivated him to strikingly exhort on Mar's Hill, God "hath made of one blood all nations of men" (Acts 17:26, KJV). Consider the pronounced fact that Paul wouldn't have been on Mar's Hill in the first place, preaching to idol worshippers, had he not had a burning belief in the sanctity and unity of all the human race.

Paul very clearly teaches the divine foundation for interracial relationships when he grittily exhorted to the Ephesian Christians:

> But now you belong to Christ Jesus, and though you once were far away from God, now you have been brought very near to him because of what Jesus Christ has done for you with his blood.
> For Christ himself is our way of peace. He has made peace between us Jews and you Gentiles by making us all one family, breaking down the wall of contempt that used to separate us. By his death he ended the angry resentment between us, caused by the Jewish laws which favored the Jews and excluded the Gentiles, for he died to annul that whole system of Jewish laws. Then he took the two groups that had been opposed to each other and made them parts of himself; thus he fused us together to become one new person, and at last there was peace. As parts of the same body, our anger against each other has disappeared, for both of us have been reconciled to God. And so the feud ended at last at the cross (Ephesians 2:13–16, *The Living Bible*).

Because so many Christians haven't yet learned, these words of Paul must continually be proclaimed—that in Christ the barriers of race, language, culture, and social class are all transcended. For man to put up these superficial fences truly reflects the superficiality of his humanity. As God informed Samuel of old, "for the Lord seeth not as man seeth; for man looketh on the outward appearance, but the Lord looketh on the heart" (I Samuel 16:7, KJV). In short, in Jesus Christ you and I become "a new creation." And as new creatures in Christ we are made for the first time truly human, truly real—in touch with ourselves and in tune with our fellowman.

The lesson on the value and dignity of all men that the prophet Jonah and other past saints learned was relearned by the apostle Peter. Bigotry deeply ingrained Peter's Jewish mentality. After his conversion to faith in Jesus Christ he experienced a gradual transformation of his steep feelings of racial superiority. To him the Gentiles were as pigs. The record of Acts 10 testifies to the power of the gospel in overcoming severe racial prejudice. After a startling vision and the extraordinary events surrounding this vision, the mysteriously changed Peter declared:

> . . . "You know it is against the Jewish laws for me to come into a Gentile home like this. But God has shown me in a vision that I should never think of anyone as inferior . . . ." Then Peter replied [again], "I see very clearly that the Jews are not God's only favorites! In every nation he has those who worship him and do good deeds and are acceptable to him (Acts 10:28, 34–35, *The Living Bible*).

If you will read the whole account as recorded by Luke in Acts 10, you may get the subtle feeling (as I did) that God took extreme measures to radically alter Peter's racial attitude. It seems as if the transforming of the apostle's prejudice was of grave concern to God and vitally important to the staggering task to which he ordained the early Christians. Every detail leading to Peter's vision, and every detail following Peter's vision suggests the meticulous planning and work of God. Could such delicate care of critical events mean anything but the absolute necessity for Peter (and for Christianity) to begin to shed his shameful attitude of racial superiority?

The lesson learned by Old and New Testament men of God must be embraced and practiced by Christians today. Racial prejudice enlivens an extremely powerful poison that enslaves everyone, Christians and non-Christians alike. It is no respecter of persons. But the sharp and penetrating medicine of the gospel can paralyze any force of evil. The racial attitude in your home, your office, your church, and your community, may largely depend on you. As that tune goes, "it just takes a spark to set a flame a glowin'."

John 3:16 reminds us plainly that the Lord is a God for every tongue and tribe. He considers all as equally worthy of salvation. That every person on earth is to be respected as God's own is magnificently reflected in many verses interspersed throughout the New Testament (Luke 2:47, Revelation 14:6). Jesus reveals the supreme will of God regarding his Kingdom family, "And they shall come from the east, and from the west, and from the north, and from the south, and shall sit down in the kingdom of God" (Luke 13:29, KJV). Also, the relevant words of Jesus in synthesizing the law and the prophets has deep implications for racism and prejudice: "Thou shalt love the Lord thy God with all thy heart, and with all thy soul, and with all thy mind. This is the first and great commandment. And the second is like unto it, Thou shalt love thy neighbor as thyself" (Matthew 22:37–39, KJV).

One day as the Spirit of God led Philip to travel southward from Jerusalem to Gaza, the apostle encountered an Ethiopian eunich "of great authority" reading from the writings of the prophet Isaiah. The Spirit "moved" Philip toward this dark stranger sitting upon his chariot. Philip inquired, "Do you understand it?" (Acts 8:30, *The Living Bible*)—and the wheel of sacred communication was spinned into motion. Philip beautifully interpreted the good news of salvation that has come in the person of Jesus Christ, and the Holy Spirit touched the sensitive nerve of belief in the African. Coming unto some water, the eunich cried out, "Look! Water! Why can't I be baptized" (Acts 8:36, *The Living*

Bible)? With that he was promptly baptized. What simplicity. What childlike faith. How we often miss today the fresh and spontaneous expressions of God's marvelous works in our all-too-often stilted religious traditions.

Now, two verses from the above conversion story are noteworthy. In Acts 8:26 we see the Lord leading Philip southward on the very road on which he later meets the Ethiopian eunich. And in verse 29 the Spirit then commanded Philip to actually brave an encounter with the stranger. Because of this bold action the stranger's life is forever changed. Not only do we see the Lord directing the apostle's journey, but it is obvious that he does so with a definite purpose—the salvation of the Ethiopian.

Something else is obvious from this encounter of two men from different ethnic backgrounds. What's the message that may help you in your encounters with those of different racial identities? Simply this, just as Philip allowed the Spirit of God to *control* his life, you must be willing to permit this same Spirit complete rule in your life. For if you do, you may then surprise yourself by being involved with ethnic personalities to such a degree that, like Philip, you will have little time worrying about the color of a man's skin. Relations with ethnic minorities may cause you to love them in spite of superficial differences. And . . . halleleuah!

Don't you agree with me that Philip must have been quite startled to catch himself conversing with an African foreigner that day? How unlikely. Yet one by one, we see the creative hands of God shaping and expanding the heart and vision of the early apostles. Don't you also agree with me that God wants to surprise *you* by the kind of love you can show to ethnic minorities?

You must want to associate with ethnic minorities. You must want to love your neighbor as you love yourself. And then, most important of all, you must *do it.*

Excuses come by as easily and naturally as the dust on your coffee table. Wanting something and actually acting upon that desire are not the same. But for those of you who give it a try, don't be too amazed if you begin to discover and relive the miracles that revolutionized the lives of Paul, Peter, Philip, and other Christian ambassadors! Be willing. Oh, what God can do with those who are simply *willing,* and courageous to *act.*

Other instances of encounters with different racial characters in the Bible will not be delineated since the treatment here is not intended to be exhaustive. However, I do hope you are stimulated enough with these accounts to be challenged to do biblical research on your own. Discover the enlightening ways in which God led men in past ages to vanquish racial pride. With a gradual or perhaps dramatic loosening of the choking grip of racial prejudice, investigate—and by all means *experience*—how God can generate a fresh and beautiful love in your life.

I challenge you.

See Individuals, Not Racial Stereotypes

This is what God does. No, God isn't oblivious of racial differences; he sees the physical distinctions. After all, he made us. And the Bible says that all he created is "good." But to him the real measure of a man's worth is spiritual, not physical. God views every individual for his own intrinsic worth. It's of no particular concern to God if a person has a nose five inches long and walks like a duck; he's still a human being created in the divine image.

Unfortunately, we don't *cherish* men the way God does. You see, if there were a people from an obscure part of the world who actually had noses five inches long and who did really walk like ducks, they would undoubtedly be the most ridiculed "race" on earth. Of course, these funny-looking people would be classified as highly inferior—surely!

We must intensely seek to capture the sense of the sacred in every individual and not allow racial stereotype and bigotry to sinisterly taint our treatment of people. And when I say "we" I mean everyone, *all* Christians, for every segment in American society embodies, to some degree, racial prejudice against others.

Let me cite an example which illustrates a facet of the universality of racial tension. I once heard a friend comment that a difficulty many missionaries encounter as they arrive in a foreign country is the problem of gaining trust among the natives of the land. This problem is heightened by the ominous cloud of anti-American feelings shared by literally thousands around the world. These waves of anti-Americanism can be better understood when one reviews the tragic history of white imperialism, the jealousy arising from the wealth of American industry abroad, and the frequently brash manner in which these Americans often behave overseas. The "Ugly American" is no myth; it's a view held on the four corners of the earth. Americans are almost spontaneously stereotyped as "rich," "racist," "freewheeling," and "spoiled." It is easy to understand, then, how unfortunate Christian missionaries are when they are called upon to work in such adverse climates.

How vicious it is when anyone is treated solely on preconception, prejudice, or stereotype! For the Christian especially he mustn't allow racial stereotyping to divert his attention from developing a healthy, loving relationship with those of other ethnic identities. As God does, you must accept every person as glittering pearls of infinite dignity.

In college I recall how my heart ached for an African friend who, upon entering a local barbershop, was nastily asked to leave because they just don't cater to "his kind." In this small Texas town where blacks fare worse than Mexican-Americans, my good friend was disgustingly told to "Get out." I haven't personally endured any such indignity, but if I had and if I wasn't a Christian I know my attitude towards Anglo-Americans would more than brush the sleeve of hatred. The sensitivities of some will not permit them to be repeatedly insulted and still maintain their mental-emotional equilibrium.

Acts 16 recounts an incident worth noting here. Being directed by the Holy Spirit to enter Macedonia, Paul went through Samothracia and Neopolis before arriving in Philippi. After several incidents Paul and Silas are found in jail, praying and singing praises to God. Weirdos, some must have thought. Abruptly at midnight a violent earthquake sprung loose the prison doors, an occurrence so dreadful the earthworms beneath the cell must have shuddered in nervous confusion. The guard keeping watch was rattled in more ways than one, for not only was he shaken out of a deep sleep but he was shaken half out of his wits as well. Fearing the escape of all the prisoners, he hurriedly rushed to see if he had cause to take his own life. But miraculously Paul reassured him "we are all here" (v. 28), at which the Philippian (Greek) fell prostrate before Paul and Silas, marveling at the calm of these men of God. After this dramatic experience, the jailor anxiously inquired about the way to salvation. Paul thrilled at the opportunity to explain to him the transforming love of Jesus Christ. This dialogue was the *real* drama.

Like Paul, we must learn to accept everyone as precious gems for whom Christ died. Although a Jew, Paul was a Christian as well, and this latter identity carried supreme preeminence over his life. That is, he attained the necessary ability (compassion) to effectively discard his prejudice and learn to dispense love toward all nationalities as "brothers" in whom divine sanctity is inherent. Paul gained the knack of looking at the man (the Greek jailor, for example), and not at the race, color, or nationality of the man.

The indescribable love Paul exuded for any Gentile is classically seen in his brief encounter with King Agrippa (Acts 26). Portius Festus, realizing the vehemence at which the Jews desired to dispose of Paul, but finding no crime to report to Caesar, dismayingly delivered Paul to King Agrippa in the hopes that he might uncover something which Festus could use in his report to the Roman emperor. When Agrippa permitted Paul to speak, the apostle began a lengthy and emotional discourse revealing the marvelous work of God through Jesus Christ in his life. The political ruler was deeply moved by Paul's sincerity. Intuitively sensing that his words were getting through to the king, Paul ended his brilliant testimony by asking: "King Agrippa, believest thou the prophets? I know that thou believest" (Acts 26:27, KJV). Agrippa movingly replied, "Paul, almost thou persuadest me to be a Christian" (Acts 26:28, KJV). To which Paul cried, "I would to God, that not only thou, but also all that hear me this day, were both almost, and altogether such as I am, except these bonds" (Acts 26:29, KJV). May God have mercy on a Christian who can't witness like Paul because of prejudice in his heart.

Some may argue that Paul was preaching only *for his neck* in the Agrippa incident. But evidence to the contrary are voluminous as one carefully acknowledges the words and deeds of Paul after his conversion experience. Aptly described as "Spirit-filled," Paul so possessed the nature and compassion of the living Christ that it is improbable he would selfishly plead for his own life before King Agrippa. He knew Christ completely controlled his life and destiny. He savored no desire to take the cowardly course of trying to save his own skin as the dominant intent of his discourse. No, Paul was not preaching for self-preservation—he was simply witnessing in love to a man, to a man in need of The Man. The divine intention of the apostle transcended his own weak humanity and released him to see a man in need of a personal experience with the Savior *of the world.*

Embody the Mind of Christ

I think it's just fantastic for a husband and wife to know each other so well that they "intuitively" know what the other is thinking or feeling without any word exchange. You understand, to achieve this "union of the minds" does not come automatically upon marriage. But in a good marriage a form of spiritual transfusion takes place. All the love and affection and intimacies and communication that a healthy marital relationship nurtures performs the miracle of "oneness." Over years of close, loving companionship both partners begin to embody (personify, incorporate) to a great degree the mind of the other.

In like manner our union with Jesus Christ is a marriage of intimate dimensions. Yet it is not a relationship between equals. You must allow Christ to live and rule within you. This transformation is called "embodying the mind of Christ." In order for you as an Anglo-American Christian to do your part in manifesting the indiscriminate love of God to ethnic minorities, you must attain the mind of Christ and engraft it into your personality. I see no distinction between the "mind" of Christ and the "spirit" of Christ, for to me they convey essentially the same idea—engrafting the character of Christ into yours. And that's saying a mouthful. An entire book can be written on the "character of Christ" and all that implies for the Christian.

Paul declares to the Corinthians, "we have the mind of Christ" (I Cor. 2:16, KJV). His explanation of the phrase is pretentiously unfolded in his preceding statements: "Now we have received, not the spirit of the world, but the spirit which is of God; that we might know the things that are freely given to us of God. Which things also we speak, not in words which man's wisdom teacheth, but which the Holy Ghost teacheth" (I Corinthians 2:12–13, KJV).

Embodying the mind of Christ is beautifully illustrated by Jesus in his teaching at a synagogue recorded in John 6. Here Jesus describes himself as the "bread of life" and says that any man who eats this bread will live forever (v. 51). Jesus replied:

> With all the earnestness I possess I tell you this: Unless you eat the flesh of the Messiah and drink his blood, you cannot have eternal life within you. But anyone who does eat my flesh and drink my blood has eternal life, and I will raise him at the Last Day. For my flesh is the true food, and my blood is the true drink. Everyone who eats my flesh and drinks my blood is in me, and I in him. I live by the power of the living Father who sent me, and in the same way those who partake of me shall live because of me! I am the true Bread from heaven; and anyone who eats this Bread shall live forever, and not die as your fathers did—though they ate bread from heaven (John 6:53–58, *The Living Bible*).

To embody the mind of Christ, then, is to allow the love, lifeblood, and vitality of Jesus to fill you and flow through you to touch the lives of others around you. Paul sweepingly dramatized this idea by urging the Corinthians "to keep the unity of the Spirit in the bond of peace. There is one body, and one Spirit, even as ye are called in one hope of your calling; One Lord, one faith, one baptism, One God a Father of all, who is above all, and through all, and in you all" (Ephesians 4:3–6, KJV).

But for people to actually become Spirit-filled and Spirit-directed constitutes a major problem. Where do you start? I can tell you *when* to start, but I can't tell you *where.* You must begin now to embody the mind of Christ. There ought to be no delay in this urgent matter. This hurting and bewildered planet demands immediacy on the part of the Christian to grow in the character of Christ. Where you begin, though, will depend on "where you are now." You must take this highly personal question and prayerfully present it to the Lord. Ask him to help you see your life in proper perspective, and begin from there. The overriding point is still: wherever you are in your Christian maturity, *begin now*—get going and initiate steps to embody the mind of Christ.

Go the Second Mile

"And whosoever shall compel thee to go a mile, go with him twain" (Matthew 5:41, KJV).

It's not easy. But then Jesus didn't say the Christian's life and task would be. To me, going the second mile simply means embodying the mind of Christ; the two are inseparable. Just as you can't have a living tree without roots, so you can't go the second mile without the mind of Christ.

At first glance "going the second mile" may imply *action,* and to possess "the mind of Christ" may imply a *condition.* That is, the former implies doing something whereas the latter implies a spiritual state or condition of the one doing the action. But I don't think we should necessarily distinguish action and condition in a distinct way. I would rather suggest that both of the above concepts represent an energetic "condition-action" balance. Let me explain this dynamic this way: "going the second mile" symbolizes a condition of a man's spiritual maturity just as "embodying the mind of Christ" represents a vibrant, growing activity within the life of the believer.

I will never forget my roommate in college. He came from Leuders, Texas, a small town not too far from Abilene. He probably never had a Japanese-American friend before he met me. I recall being extremely apprehensive in going to the panhandle of Texas to begin a college career. But the ready acceptance and love Douglas displayed toward me is a keen impression permanently sealed within my heart.

So many times Douglas went out of his way to talk to me about my problems. Upon first arriving on campus I didn't bring much with me, only a limited amount of clothes, shoes, and other essentials. In fact, I had only one suitcase. I distinctly remember Douglas saying to me, on more than one occasion, "Nelson, whatever I have is yours." He meant it. He demonstrated it. I was quickly convinced he cared *for me*.

Since I didn't own a car at the time, he frequently took me to the store, to the barbershop, to church, home with him—all without ever showing signs of resentment. He was proud of the fact that I was his roommate. I recall clearly how he used to brag about me before friends, always speaking fondly of his Japanese-American "roomie." He was generous with his possessions, his time, and his love. I grew to understand the meaning of Christian love as a direct result of his life, a life pulsating the spirit of Christ. How fortunate I am to have lived with Douglas in Brotherhood Hall, Wayland Baptist College. At a time when I needed him most, he was there. He was God's man for me at that point in my life.

I urge you, I plead with you, to embody the mind of Jesus our Lord so that your life will exude the love of God, a love which always pursues the second mile, even with ethnic minorities.